M000107771

faithfully *Yours* WORSHIPFUL DEVOTIONS FROM THE PSALMS

AS HIGH AS THE HEAVENS

DAVID M. EDWARDS

BROADMAN & HOLMAN PUBLISHERS

NASHVILLE, TENNESSEE

AS HIGH AS THE HEAVENS
Faithfully Yours: Worshipful Devotions from the Psalms, Book 3
Copyright © 2006 by David M. Edwards
All Rights Reserved

ISBN 0-8054-4331-2
ISBN 13: 978-0-8054-4331-8
Broadman & Holman Publishers
Nashville, Tennessee
www.broadmanholman.com

Unless otherwise noted, all Scripture quotations have been taken from the
Holman Christian Standard Bible® Copyright © 1999, 2000, 2002, 2003 by
Holman Bible Publishers.

Dewey Decimal Classification: 242
Devotional Literature \ Worship

Printed in China
1 2 3 4 09 08 07 06

foreword

The Psalms represent the span of humanity at its best and worst. That's why I return to them almost daily, and have for the past thirty years.

Joy, tragedy, complaint and supplication—it's all there. Having the opportunity to dissect these poems and songs alone has been a delight, but having a pastor to illuminate them in fresh ways has been even better.

While working on the music counterpart to this manuscript with David M. Edwards, I had the opportunity to do just that. In this book, David clearly and directly dissects the Psalms with simple concepts that will minister to all.

From the cry for cleansing in Psalm 51 to rehearsing God's magnificence in Psalm 8, there is a distinct communiqué between the created and the Creator. The psalmist is asking, "Show me how to love You better. Clear my life of hindrances and grow me in Your light. Teach me how to worship You in all I do, in all my ways."

May this book empower you on your journey towards a lifestyle of worship.

—Margaret Becker

Lay any burden upon me; only sustain me.
Send me anywhere; only go with me.
Sever any tie, but that one
which binds me to Thy service
and to Thy heart.

—David Livingstone, Scottish missionary to Africa (1813–1873)

to elyse,
daddy loves you.

introduction

For thousands of years the Psalms have been the hymnbook of Israel and the Church. Untold millions have been ministered to by their words of comfort, hope, and healing. The writers of the Psalms, primarily King David, led of the Holy Spirit, penned words that run the gamut of human emotion and experience. For instance, one minute we're reading David's triumphant words of victory and shouts of praise to God and the next we see him running for his life and begging for God's deliverance.

It is this that draws us and keeps us coming back for more because we can see our own lives lived out in the extremes of this language of the soul. Every sentence exudes the raw feelings we all have when it comes to processing life. We can so readily identify with David's temptations, struggles, failures, and sin as well his desire to confess, be forgiven, and be made whole. These stories are our stories and this is why these Psalms are so dear to us. There is no doubt that God designed each one to minister life to us.

The common thread throughout this collection of "praise songs" is exactly that: worship! The consistent and constant unifying theme is worship. These Psalms teach us that no matter what we're going through, no matter how bleak things may appear, no matter how many times we have failed God and others, we mustn't stop worshiping. Even when things don't make sense—worship. Even when we have sinned horribly in God's sight—worship. Even when we are being treated unjustly—worship.

Reading and praying these Psalms in our own spiritual journey helps keep us sensitive to God's voice and reminds us of the importance of our praise of the Holy. God loves to hear us praise Him. He hungers for our worship and desires to spend time with us. One can only imagine the countless times these ancient words have become the vehicle to access the presence of the Ancient of Days. They are timeless and eternal because He is!

My prayer is that you will find comfort, hope, and healing contained in these pages and that God the Holy Spirit will minister life to you as we look at these ancient texts. Like you, I am a fellow traveler trying to keep my ears tuned to His voice and my heart fixed on Him. Together may we remain, "Faithfully Yours."

as high as the heavens

psalm 103

My soul, praise the Lord, and all that is within me, praise
His holy name. My soul, praise the Lord, and do not
forget all His benefits.

Maybe it's just me, but each time I look out an airplane window and up into the skies, I have a strange sense of feeling closer physically to God. I know He lives in my heart. I know His Holy Spirit is within me, but there is just something about the proximity factor that gives me goose bumps!

What is it about heights that causes us to think about the *bigness* of God? I think it must be because we know he's "up there"—wherever "up there" is. As David wrote long, long ago, "For as high as the heavens are above the earth, so great is His faithful love toward those who fear Him" (verse 11).

Certainly, David wrote these words long before mankind knew of such things as interstellar space, black holes, star nurseries, or superclusters—long before we learned that objects we once thought were just stars are actually entire galaxies—long before the Hubble Telescope began daily transmitting pictures back to Earth of what lies beyond the tiny speck we live on. Even by the time we view these images from space—snapshots delivered at the speed of light—they are already history. Yet as a long-ago shepherd, knowing so much less about the universe than we do today, David had learned how to read the alignment of the planets and stars to discern the seasons. His eyes had gazed upon the same Jupiter and Mars we can see from our own backyard.

So he had to wonder—even as we still wonder—just how high are the heavens?

As we try to fathom it, we realize with breathtaking awe that God is bigger than we ever dreamed. He is more vast—"higher"—than the sum of His creation. With every new bit of information scientists discover about what is out there, I'm reminded that He is the great "I AM." There is no need to measure the heavens, for we will never find its farthest reaches. They are as endless as their Creator.

But just as endless is His love for each one of us! His constant, consistent love towards those who honor and respect Him is as immeasurable as the heavens above us. There is no end to His love. It is eternal!

Psalm 103 declares it. It is full of God's unchanging majesty, making profound declarations of His mercy. In it we discover how God forgives all our sin, how He heals us, redeems us, and crowns us with love and compassion (verses 3–5). Regardless of our humanness, our iniquity, our mistake-prone condition, we can still receive pardon and mercy at the foot of His throne.

In fact, when we recognize our sin, when we come to Him repenting of it, He mercifully removes our sin from us "as far as the east is from the west" (verse 12). Like the heavens, we cannot measure the distance between east and west or pinpoint their locations on a map. It is a divine conundrum! Our confessed sin is simply vaporized by the blood of Jesus. When God says He has removed it, we just need to walk in the assurance of that fact.

Therefore, as believers in the Lord God Jehovah, you and I are charged today with the duty of remembering all these "benefits." Never take God's positive track record of blessing in your life for granted! Even in the worst of circumstances—*especially* in the worst of circumstances—recount the ways He has blessed and provided for you. Build up your faith by reminding yourself of what He has led you through before, and praise Him that He will do it again!

Furthermore, we are warned about an insidious danger—the danger of *forgetting* what God has done for us. One of the worst offenses to God is the sin of ingratitude, which stems from pride. We must not forget His blessings! We need to remind ourselves daily that God has never failed us and never will!

Thank Him and honor Him for all of His wonderful works. Give Him glory for saving you and filling you with His Holy Spirit. Exalt Him for His Word that will not pass away. Extol Him for His great faithful love toward you. Praise His name . . . "as high as the heavens!"

as high as the heavens

Verse 1
My soul, praise the Lord
And all that is within me
Praise His holy name
Do not forget
All of His benefits
And healing strength

Chorus
For as high as the heavens
Are above the earth
So great is His faithful love
And as far as the east is
From the west
He has removed our sins
From us, from us

Verse 2
My soul, praise the Lord
He forgives your sins
And redeems your life
He crowns you with love
And everlasting goodness
He will satisfy

Written by Margaret Becker & David M. Edwards. ©2004 Modern M/SESAC. Admin. by Music Services, Inc.
Van Ness Press/ASCAP. Admin. by LifeWay Worship Music Group.

the lord is my shepherd

psalm 23

The Lord is my shepherd; there is nothing I lack. He lets me lie
down in green pastures; He leads me beside quiet waters.

One of my earliest memories is of a Warner Sallman framed print called "The Good Shepherd" that hung in my grandmother's house. It was a painting of Jesus carrying a lamb in one arm and holding a staff with his other hand. Around his feet and trailing behind him was a flock of sheep.

Sallman's worship art touched my heart at a very young age and left an indelible impression on me as to what God is like. His painting embodies our relationship with the Lord. Sometimes we are the little lamb, void of strength, carried in His arms. Sometimes we are strong enough to walk on our own, but never far from the Shepherd.

And in David's most famous psalm—Psalm 23—we discover the consummate picture of our very own Shepherd, whose tender, loving care is ever near.

David had known life as both a shepherd and as a sheep in God's flock. I'm sure that's one of the reasons he made such a great king. The words he wrote were taken from his own first-hand experiences.

He knew that it is the job of a shepherd to provide for those entrusted to his care. The sheep's food, water, and protection are his responsibility and focus. Even while they pasture or sleep, the shepherd's mind is already thinking ahead about what to do next. His sheep are dependent upon him to meet their every need—no exceptions. When they move, they are not just following a man. They are following their source of survival!

For us, Jesus Himself is our Shepherd. And since He is our source and supply, we will never want for anything as long as we continue to follow and serve Him. Jesus truly is the wellspring of life.

We enter this world from the darkness of our mother's womb, and within seconds we are introduced to light. As children we equate light with safety. The light helps us see our way and keeps us from stumbling.

Most of us probably checked beneath our bed or opened our closet doors when we were young, just to make sure there were no monsters lurking about. While that may seem immature and silly looking back on it, we realize as we grow older that monsters are real. They come in the form of sickness, disease, broken marriages, financial ruin, torn lives, depression, divided relationships, even death. And with them comes a pervading darkness that is unsettling, a fear that tries its best to wear down our faith in the Almighty.

Thankfully, though, we have a Shepherd standing in the shadows!

The same God who was with you in the darkness of your mother's womb is with you in the darkness you face now. He has never left your side. Your Shepherd reaches out His hand and says, "It's okay . . . we'll go together!"—through dark valleys, yes, but always with Someone's hand to hold on to!

If you follow this Good Shepherd, He will always lead you to places of great joy and safety. He will even provide a victory dinner in your honor, to be seen by the very ones who sought your demise, preparing "a table before [you] in the presence of [your] enemies" (verse 5). As David said in another place, "Many will see and fear, and put their trust in the Lord" (Psalm 40:3), standing in awe of the way He delivers His people.

This is what a real Shepherd does. He doesn't run away at the first sign of trouble. He delivers you because He loves you. He has not walked with you through all of life's ups and downs to cut out on you now.

The ultimate reward, however, for any of us who follow Jesus Christ is the joy of being with Him forever and ever! His goodness and mercy that follow alongside us all our days on this side of heaven will one day lead us straight into His arms in glory.

Thus, the circle will be complete. The God who was with you before you were formed, whose voice you heeded and followed on earth, who walked with you every step of the way, is the God who will welcome you into His house to live forever. There will be no more dark valleys, no more hills to climb, no more enemies to face. And the only tears will be tears of joy that He will brush away with His nail-scarred hands, the hands of a Shepherd.

i'd rather dwell

psalm 84

How lovely is Your dwelling place, Lord of Hosts. . . .

Better a day in Your courts than a thousand anywhere else.

Have you ever heard someone say, "I grew up in church" or "I was raised in church"? For those of us who grew up in a minister's home, that's not too far from the truth. We were the first ones to arrive at the church and the last ones to leave after each service and event. Many a Saturday my brother and I would play in and around the church while our parents went about their duties.

This developed in me a deep love and respect for the church—God's house—and for the work of His ministers. I understood that all of the preparation and "behind the scenes" work had one purpose: to see God's glory and Presence show up when we gathered so that lives would be touched, changed, and healed.

I loved being in His Place. It didn't matter if I was taking out the trash or singing a song. I just loved being there. There was something about it—the place where heaven and earth met. Things man could not do were made possible in His Place. There was always such hope and expectation because we knew that nothing was too difficult for God.

Whatever you needed, He had the answer.

He *was* the answer!

Psalm 84 shows that King David, too, had a deep affection and affinity for God's house and what took place there. These are some of the most tender and heartfelt words in all of the Bible about wanting to spend time with God. This psalm was written by a true worshiper, someone who understood that there is nothing more important in the universe than being in God's abiding Presence.

Truly, the "dwelling place" of the Lord is a place of refuge where we are protected and provided for. Even the word *sanctuary* still carries with it the ancient connotation of asylum and safety. From the smallest to the greatest, from the most plain to the most elaborate and ornate, God's House is a haven for those whose hearts are set on Him. In God's Presence we can reside in the glow of His love without fear or worry.

Furthermore, we should not neglect the admonishment of verse 3 to raise our children near His altar. The worship of God should be ever-present in our homes, and the sweet smell of sacrifice should be a familiar fragrance to our kids. Moms and dads need to model a lifestyle of surrender to God's will, God's way, and God's Word. It is our great privilege as parents to lead our children to His Throne in both prayer and praise.

Have you ever said, "If I had a million dollars I would do this or that"? We know deep down, though, that all the money in the world could never buy us what we really need. Money can't buy His "grace and glory" (verse 11). It can't buy an answer to prayer, a measure of His strength, or the peaceful touch of His closeness. God's nearness is a priceless privilege reserved only for those who praise Him continually and put their trust in Him.

The psalmist is telling us, "If the closest I can get to You are the church steps, Lord, I'll take it. I'd rather be there than live at a distance any day. If all I get to do is hold the door open for everyone else, I'll take it. I need you more than anything else in my life!"

This is the cry of the hungry soul, pouring out our hearts to the Lord, recognizing that there is nothing more valuable than a relationship with God Almighty!

It is His Presence we hunger for.

What good is the building or structure if He's not there? This is not about the building. It's all about longing for Him, far beyond where the door is located. Wherever He is, that's where I want to be!

Under the Old Covenant, God loved His people from behind a veil and through the smoky sacrifices offered on His altars. But through the sending of His One and Only Son, Jesus Christ, His "dwelling place" moved from a fixed physical structure to the hearts of people who cry out for the living God. Jesus' blood has paved the way for you to enter His holy Presence. Lift your hands, lift your heart, and enter in!

god alone

psalm 62

I am at rest in God alone; my salvation comes from Him.

He alone is my rock and my salvation, my stronghold;

I will never be shaken.

Four times in this passionate psalm, David declared that God "alone" is our all sufficiency. What a faith declaration! What a testimony! There is no need to look anywhere else for what we need. He is it!

These are not the words of a spiritual novice. They come to us from someone who had been through some serious stuff—threats, lies, false accusation, gossip, and slander (verses 3–4). Many of us carry the same scars. We've learned the hard way that nothing is worse than a hypocritical relationship that simulates loyalty but would turn on you in a minute.

David understood what that was like. He had suffered much from verbal attacks, and he knew the toll they had taken on him, mentally and physically. So his testimony encourages all of us, not just because he had come through it but because he let us know how he did it:

"God alone!"

Only God can lead us in, lead us out, and lead us on. There is no other place of safety or source of hope. In fact, this psalm makes it clear that while we are resting in "God alone," we are at the same time being strengthened within. Our spirits are being disciplined to hold fast and trust.

Twice the psalmist declared that he would not be "shaken." This again is the voice of experience, strengthening the resolve of those who might be tempted to give up or give in. It is one man taking his painful experiences and the faith lessons he's learned along the way, and using them all to encourage us—to help us take a stand, trust in God, rest in His faithful love, and *not be shaken*!

"Trust in Him at all times, you people; pour out your hearts before Him. God is our refuge" (verse 8). This relationship between the Lord and us should be day-by-day and minute-by-minute, not just something we try to patch up and reconnect when things are falling apart. How it must grieve God's heart when we come to Him during a time of need yet quickly meander off after the coast is clear. How well we should know that most of the things that preoccupy our lives are fleeting and empty—riches, fame, position, power, prestige. We cannot stake our eternal life on any of them.

We can only trust in one absolute: "God alone!" And in that trust we can come before Him and "pour out" our hearts.

Praise the Lord for the freedom that comes from prayer. This is the place where we should go to unburden our heart's concerns and cares. He wants to hear them. He doesn't want us going to someone else with the things that bother us. He wants us to come to Him, to trust Him.

Both power and mercy come from God. He is their source (verses 11–12). Only He has the ability to deliver us, the right to extend and grant forgiveness to the penitent. God is the only One who can protect us and love us like no other. He is our Heavenly Father and He is passionate about His kids!

This psalm closes with a sobering reminder: "You repay each according to his works" (verse 12). We know that our salvation is not by works for we are saved by grace through faith. However, the result of our salvation and Christianity should be lives of service to the King of kings, extending His love to others. If I want to reap God's blessings and touch on my life, then I need to make sure my actions and my speech lines up with His holy Word.

If we would but rest in God, we would find a place of abiding that cannot be shaken. No matter what things may look like, no matter how dark the day may get or how long the night may seem to drag on, God is still our rock, our stronghold, our refuge, and our salvation! The only way not to be shaken is to be found in Him alone!

god alone

Chorus
I am at rest in God alone
My salvation comes from God alone
He alone is my rock
And all my glory
I will never be
Shaken

Verse 1
Life is just a vapor
But God will always be
His faithful love and glory
Endures eternally

Verse 2
Pour out your hearts before Him
Trust in Him always
Let all the earth bear witness
To God belongs the strength

Written by Margaret Becker & David M. Edwards. ©2005 Modern M/SESAC. Admin. by Music Services, Inc. Van Ness Press/ASCAP. Admin. by LifeWay Worship Music Group.

this god, our god

psalm 48

The Lord is great and highly praised in the city of our God. His
holy mountain, rising splendidly, is the joy of the whole earth.

Psalm 48 was written to celebrate one of the greatest military victories of all time. King Sennacherib of Assyria was intent on destroying Jerusalem and its inhabitants. So he sent a letter to Judah's godly king, Hezekiah, to warn him of impending doom, instructing him to surrender—or else! Sennacherib foolishly proclaimed, "Don't let your God, whom you trust, deceive you by promising that Jerusalem will not be handed over to the king of Assyria" (2 Kings 19:10).

King Hezekiah took this evil letter into God's Presence and laid it before Him, pouring out his heart to the God he loved and trusted. And God answered Hezekiah's concerns: "He [Sennacherib] will not enter this city. . . . I will defend this city and rescue it for My sake" (2 Kings 19:32, 34).

God was true to His word. The night before the battle, He sent an angel against the Assyrian army, and 185,000 men were killed overnight. When the people of Jerusalem awoke in the morning, they looked out on both a horrific and wonderful scene. God had fought for them again and gained them the victory!

That's because the walls of Jerusalem were not Israel's first lines of defense. Neither was her army or the city's strategic geographical position. Her first and only line of defense was God and God alone! He had promised to wipe out the enemy, and that's exactly what He did! It didn't matter how big the Assyrian army was. What mattered then—and what matters still—is that the Lord God Jehovah is bigger than any enemy His people face.

So we don't need to waste our energy answering the taunts of the enemy or exchanging diplomatic favors to see if we can forestall the conflict. We just need to take the threats of the enemy—and whatever else is bothering us—and go directly to God with it. Like Hezekiah of old, we need to lay it all out before our Heavenly Father and pour out our heart of concern.

He wants to hear from us. He wants to know what we're concerned about. He cares and He loves us more than anything in this world. Tell Him all about it.

Our enemy, like Sennacherib, will think, "This will be easy! They have no apparent signs of defense, no strength to fight a protracted siege. It's just a matter of time and they'll be finished." But the enemy can't prepare for what he cannot see. There's no way of knowing when or how your Secret Weapon is going to strike.

And by the time God has acted, it's too little, too late for your foe. Hallelujah! What God did for Hezekiah, He will do for you and me. He will deliver us out of the hands of the enemy. You can go ahead and start worshiping Him—*before the battle ever starts*—because He will assuredly give you the victory!

Let's not allow our emotions to succumb to whatever hellish hullabaloo is coming over the wall. Instead, let's take up battle positions on our knees, with hands outstretched to the One worthy of all glory, honor, and praise! There is no place on this earth where God's hand cannot reach you, pick you up, and pull you out! God can right the wrong, make the crooked place straight, and cause rough terrain to become smooth beneath your feet.

Truly, His praise fills the atmosphere around the globe as millions upon millions of His children offer up thanksgiving for each and every answered prayer and victory won. A symphony of worship rises through Earth's atmosphere as He is enthroned in the praises of those who love Him.

What must it sound like in heaven? What must it sound like to the angels? And what must it sound like in hell? His Name alone is magnified above the heavens!

Next time the enemy sends you a threatening letter or shouts his anti-hope rhetoric over the wall of your soul, run straight into God's Presence, fall on your knees, pour out your heart, and worship! Remember all that He's done for you before. He didn't bring you this far to leave you alone. Take a good look at where He's brought you from and where you'd be if He hadn't intervened. Look again at how big God is. And how small the size of your enemy.

at all times

psalm 34

I will praise the Lord at all times; His praise will always
be on my lips. I will boast in the Lord; the humble will
hear and be glad.

The New Testament writers seemed to love quoting from Psalm 34. Maybe its one-liners are so memorable because they poured forth from a man who was desperate, broken, and undone, like we are so often.

David wrote this psalm as he remembered yet another time when he had run for his life trying to get away from King Saul's jealous rage. This time, however, he had fled into enemy territory to get away. Quickly realizing his mistake, he had feigned madness to get out.

There are four verses from this psalm underlined in my Bible, because these ancient words play an important part in my walk with the Lord. They have often breathed life into me when I was weary, battle worn, and hungry for something only God could give.

"I will praise the Lord at all times; His praise will always be on my lips" (verse 1).

This is one of my life's anthems. I say it every morning in order to set the spiritual tone for the day. Many of us are complaining before we ever get out of bed in the morning. Some of us even start the night before! But we need to make this faith declaration regardless of how we are feeling. This is one way to train your spirit-man to speak before your flesh does.

I refuse to be a fair-weather friend of Jesus and only praise Him when I feel like it! My praise to God should not be mitigated by outside influences and circumstances. He ought to be able to depend upon my praise.

"I sought the Lord, and He answered me and delivered me from all my fears" (verse 4).

We each know how a care can become a concern; a concern, a worry; and a worry, a controlling "spirit of fear" (2 Tim. 1:7). The devil loves to use fear to trick us into making rash and hasty decisions based on emotion rather than on what God would have us do. But when faced with these types of circumstances, the formula in this verse is clear and sure. Take your burden to the Lord first. His heart of love and compassion will answer back, and His arms of salvation will bring about a mighty deliverance. He will set us free from "all" our fears when we cast our cares on Him.

"Taste and see that the Lord is good. How happy is the man who takes refuge in Him (verse 8).

One taste of the Lord and nothing else will satisfy! There is no substitute for a relationship with Jesus. This is why it is so important for people to be exposed to God's Presence. If they could just encounter Jesus and His healing love, their desire for sin and other wasting pleasures would begin to diminish, because these cannot offer what He can.

Those of us who have tasted and experienced Jesus Christ's Presence realize that He has ruined us for another's love. The happiness we find from being hidden in Him cannot be duplicated or manufactured. He alone is the only source of goodness and true contentment.

"The Lord is near the brokenhearted; He saves those crushed in spirit" (verse 18).

I'll never forget sitting in a restaurant with a pastor friend of mine, trying to relay to him the pain I felt over a spiritual battle I had been in—and was still going through. I shared with him how

I could no longer verbalize the pain I had obviously underestimated in my life.

Furthermore, I was embarrassed by my own inability to handle this on my own as God's man of faith and power. I was equating the length of the battle with some kind of weakness on my part.

He looked at me and said, "A man's spirit can endure sickness, but who can survive a broken spirit?" (Proverbs 18:14). "David," he whispered, "your spirit has been crushed." As tears ran down my cheeks, I was reminded again that God had not left me. His Presence was still there, sustaining me. I was being trained for something greater, something I couldn't see at the time. And though my spirit was crushed, I knew He would save and restore.

When life's circumstances are crushing your spirit, know that the Lord is near, ready to save and heal. Jesus specializes in mending broken things, especially when it's you and me.

this is the day

psalm 118

This is the day the Lord has made; let us rejoice and be glad
in it. . . . You are my God, and I will give you thanks. You are
my God; I will exalt You.

Psalm 118 is the last of what are called the "Hallel" psalms (short for *hallelujah*) sung at the Passover. This is the last one to be sung after the meal is over, thus it was probably the last praise and worship song sung by Jesus before His arrest and crucifixion as he ate the Passover with his disciples.

As I read these words, I wonder what Jesus must have felt as He sang them, knowing in His heart what was about to happen.

This psalm is filled with prophetic passages about the Lamb of God: his triumphal entry into Jerusalem (verses 19–20, 25-26), His agony in Gethsemane (verses 5–7), His crucifixion (verses 10–13), His victorious resurrection (verses 14–18), and His glorification, second coming, and millennial reign (verses 19–29).

And it all begins with this: "Give thanks to the Lord, for He is good; His faithful love endures forever" (verse 1). These are the foundation stones in building an altar of praise and worship to God: "He is good" and "His mercy endures forever!"

When was the last time you asked God to forgive you and He said, "Sorry, fresh out of mercy today"? Never—because His mercies are brand new every day, because goodness is not just something He does; He is goodness personified. He is the origin of all that is good. He owns the patent!

Whenever we are distressed, oppressed—even depressed—the enemy of our souls does his very best to create a claustrophobic environment of fear and heaviness. We cry out to God for release. Our spirits hunger for a place where they can breathe deeply—a place where the expanse of His Presence is felt and known.

God does indeed answer those kinds of prayers and takes us to a place where we can run free in the wide, open fields of His mercy and grace. God's blessings are big, and when He does something He does it big. So as you begin to feel the heated breath of the enemy inching closer, call upon your great and mighty Savior. He will step in and raise a standard against the enemy, moving you to a place where you can see for miles and miles.

That's the kind of God we serve! He will answer if you call. "The Lord is my strength and my song; He has become my salvation" (verse 14). There is something about a song that pulls us through and speaks to our situation. When we receive the strength of the Lord, our human spirits are buoyed by the confidence that His strength gives, and it makes us want to praise and worship Him. That's why songs are so powerful. They can transport us to a different dimension both spiritually and mentally. When God is the source of our song, it has a profound effect upon our lives and our faith.

Have you ever had times in your life when you were going through a protracted spiritual battle or a seemingly never-ending series of negative events, and you wondered how you'd ever make it through? And yet somehow you got beyond it and looked back in amazement, wondering what happened?

The Lord was your strength. You knew *you* didn't have the strength—but He did—and does! God will speak life into us when the enemy's lies are telling us we're finished.

So we need to have hearts that rejoice and worship Him at all times and in all things. We need to begin praising Him in the morning and sustain that praise all day long, thanking Him before we close our eyes at night. Each day is a brand new opportunity to praise Him, to bless His great Name, to invoke His mighty Presence to come and attend our way.

This psalm begins and ends with the very same words, "Give thanks to the Lord, for He is good; His faithful love endures forever." They are bookends that cap off a whole lot of territory in between. We will all go through things we'd rather not. We will all face times that put our faith to the test. No question about it.

But our key to victory will be making sure those times are sandwiched in between our praise to the Lord. As long as we are giving thanks before, during, and after our struggles, we'll be all right . . . because His faithful love will never end.

this is the day

Chorus
This is the day that the
Lord has made
I will rejoice and be glad in it
This is the day that the
Lord has made
I will rejoice and be glad

Verse 1
From the womb of the morning
A new day dawns
Creation bows before You
In universal song
Future, ancient, holy
Hear this offering
As I come to worship
With my everything

Verse 2
Ever-present fragrance
That fills each day
You stir my soul with wonder
In the color of your ways
Creator, Sovereign, Worthy
Hear this offering
As I come to worship
With my everything

Bridge
I will rejoice—in spite of everything
I will rejoice—whatever comes my way
I will rejoice—giving you the praise
I will rejoice—lifting high Your name

Written by David M. Edwards. ©2005 Van Ness Press/ASCAP. Admin. by LifeWay Worship Music Group.

hidden in you

psalm 61

God, hear my cry; pay attention to my prayer. I call to You
from the ends of the earth when my heart is without strength.
Lead me to a rock that is high above me.

How many times have you heard someone say, "I need to get away" or "I need a change of scenery"? People spend thousands of dollars looking for a place where they can be safe, secure, refreshed, and recharged.

Each one of us needs a spiritual place to hide, to get away and rest. When we're going through something emotionally wrenching or mind wearying, we need a hiding place right in the middle of the battlefield. Is it possible? Is there such a thing? Does it exist?

Yes!

These verses reveal four different kinds of hiding places that God becomes to those in need: a rock high above, a strong tower, a tent, and sheltering wings.

First, a rock. In the southwestern United States, Native American cliff dwellers once built their homes on the heights of mesas and canyon walls. These homes in the sky were difficult to access and therefore easy to defend. This is the image that first comes to mind for me when I think of God as "a rock that is high above me." When we are weary and worn, we can cry out to the Lord, and He will lead us to a rock beyond the reach of any enemy. No intruder will be able to access the heights made available to us on wings of faith. God will give us the strength to mount up and soar to places He has prepared for us—places where we can find rest on higher ground.

Second, a strong tower. In ancient times, a city's defensive strength was measured by the size of her ramparts and walls. The thicker and higher the walls and towers, the more formidable the city was. So when enemies approached, all the villagers sought refuge within the walls. From its towers, the defenders could see the coming attacks and act accordingly.

God is the "strong tower" that the enemy will have to face before he can get to you! He will keep you in the safety of His defenses as He wars against that which seeks to destroy you. Yes, Jesus is the Prince of Peace, but He is also the Mighty Warrior and the Lion of Judah! He has promised never to leave you or forsake you. Put your trust in your Strong Tower!

Next, a tent. This tent David referred to was not just somewhere to camp out. It was God's tent, His "Tabernacle of Meeting." This is where He dwelt, where His glory showed up, where He consumed the sacrifice, where He spoke to His people. This wasn't just any tent—this was the dwelling place of Jehovah!

And this is where we should long to live and abide—to "sit enthroned before God forever" (verse 7)—even on this side of heaven. We don't have to wait until we die to experience Him. If God manifested Himself in such demonstrative ways from the inside of a tent under the Old Covenant, how much more will His glory show up in a life totally yielded to Him under the New Covenant in Jesus' blood?

Finally, the shelter of His wings. Like the shepherd metaphor, the thought of God protecting us beneath His wings is a powerful mental picture that reveals His tenderness and His desire to nurture us. As chicks are hidden beneath the wings of their mothers for safety, they are also fed and cared for close to the mother's breast. Where would any of us be without the shielding love of heaven's wings? As believers, we have the privilege to "take refuge" there and experience His total provision "under the shelter of [His] wings" (verse 4).

I like the way this psalm closes, with a promise from us to the Lord: "I will continually sing of Your name, fulfilling my vows day by day" (verse 8). The key to all of this and the challenge to our flesh is that one word—*continually*. Yes, I know it's easier said than done, but you know what? You can start right now.

Whether you are fighting full of faith in the trenches today or you are battle worn from the struggle, keep living to honor the Lord. Keep the melody alive.

give the lord glory

psalm 29

Give the Lord—you heavenly beings—give the Lord glory and
strength. Give the Lord the glory due His name; worship the
Lord in the splendor of His holiness.

How exactly do we "give" God glory? Is it something we hand Him? Is it something we possess that we can bring to Him? These are perfectly honest questions to ask if we are to worship Him as we are instructed to do in this psalm.

But rather than giving something tangible or physical, David is telling us to "ascribe" glory to the Lord. *Ascribe* means to attribute or assign something, to "lay it at someone's door."

The two most obvious ways to ascribe all glory, strength, and honor to God is first through our *speech*—both public and private words that flow out of hearts full of love for Him. We declare these things in our personal prayer and praise time, but also when we are gathered with other believers or when witnessing to those who do not yet believe.

We also give Him glory through our *actions*—expressions of worship and obedience that emanate from lives loyally dedicated to Jesus Christ. Even the simplest or most humble acts, done in God's strength and to bring honor to Him, are ways we can give

Him glory as we worship Him in the beauty of who He is and all that He has done.

He deserves it. He is worthy of it. He is over all.

One of the most amazing sights to see is viewing a thunderstorm from an airplane. The people living below the thunder and lightning cannot see the calm above the clouds where the sun is shining and blue skies are all about, where God is commanding and controlling what lies beneath the storm from His throne high above it. And though we go through some frightening times as believers, we too can dwell in God above the storm, knowing that He is in charge, that He has promised to give us His "strength" and bless us with "peace" (verse 11).

Naturally our attention is drawn to what we see with our physical eyes and hear with our ears. But spiritually we need to realize that our Heavenly Father is above all of this, and He alone can give us peace in the midst of the raging tempest. Storms are inevitable, but God is eternal. There are blue skies beyond and the sun will shine again.

Years ago my father gave me a framed print of a dove flying aloft over an angry sea. The anonymous quote beneath it reads, "Sometimes the Lord calms the storm. Sometimes He lets the storm rage . . . and calms His child." He gave me this when I was going through a storm that refused to let up. I was giving all of my energy and concentration to the storm rather than God. I was praying for God to silence the storm, but He wanted to shelter me in the midst of it, to give me a peace that would teach me a lesson about His love for me.

Just like the precious Holy Spirit that brooded over the face of the deep prior to Creation, God is above the chaos. He took up a position above the waters and made something happen.

And this same precious Holy Spirit will brood over the empty chaos in our lives, hover over the storm, and cause something to happen! The same Lord that sat above the raging waters while Noah and his family were tossed about in a boat is the same Lord who sits above every storm you and I will ever face. He is King forever, and He will not abandon those who love Him, those who call on His mighty name. We must lift our gaze beyond what we can see and take comfort in the truth that He is still in charge.

No wonder the wind and waves obeyed Jesus when He walked the earth. They knew that voice! They had heard it many times. They knew what so many people don't—that He is the God of all creation. He spoke and it happened. Everything is subject to Him, for He is Lord of lords.

His voice is powerful at times. It can strip varnish off a wall and snap a sequoia in two. As David wrote, God's voice often "flashes," "shakes," "strips," "breaks," and "thunders." Yet He also whispers gently to our hearts, "Peace, be still."

Let those of us "in His temple all cry, 'Glory'!"

i will thank the lord

psalm 9

I will thank the Lord with all my heart; I will declare all Your
wonderful works. I will rejoice and boast about You; I will sing
about Your name, Most High.

Half-hearted worship never cuts it. We know when we're faking it, and He does too. How disconcerting it must be to God when we offer up blemished and second-hand sacrifices. We need to offer up the best to Him.

True worship takes place when we respond to Him with "all" of our heart, mind, soul, and strength. Anything less is out of line with what He deserves. So we need thankful hearts, grateful hearts, to keep us humble and broken before Him, to declare His "wonderful works" in a world where God is blamed for everything under the sun that's gone wrong and where human achievement is arrogantly applauded. He is the Creator, the Originator of all that is, and the Architect of man. We need to give God the credit that is due His great Name!

When we're bragging on God and what He's done for us (which is perfectly right and good), then we're not talking about ourselves or how important we are—or think we are. As a pastor, I never referred to the church where I ministered as "my church" because it's His Church. Often we talk about the things we do by referring to them as what "my ministry is" rather than "the ministry He's given me."

Now you might be thinking, "That's a bit extreme, isn't it?" But I want to give God the glory and credit as much as I can, never laying claim to something that's His. We are representatives of the Shepherd King, who modeled for us a life of giving God the glory! Christ's earthly ministry was never conducted in a circus atmosphere that featured select personalities. He simply functioned in His calling and loved everyone He came into contact with. His humility and brokenness were attractive to people who were fed up with religious types, those who liked everyone to know how important they were.

That's because knowing God and knowing about God are two totally different things. I know a lot of people by name that I have never met. I can read articles about them and know things about their lives. But I have people in my life with whom I have a relationship and a history. I know things about them that others who only know their name don't know.

When Jesus came into the world, He was all about one thing: re-establishing the relationship between God and man that had been torn apart by sin. It meant Jesus' death on the cross, pouring out His life's blood in order to make this possible. But He didn't do it just so we could know Him by name. He did it so that you and I could have a relationship with Him.

Be careful, loved one, to make sure that you know more about God than just His name. Those that truly "know" Him are the same ones who "seek" Him, the ones He has promised never to abandon.

Many people today are worshiping a God they don't even know, thinking they are saved merely by hanging around the accoutrements of worship. But God has a disdain for lukewarm and long-distance worship.

He wants "all" our hearts.

Not sure how to do that? It doesn't hurt to remember where you were and the condition you were in when He found you and saved you. It doesn't hurt to think about where you'd be today without Him in your life. It doesn't hurt to stop in the middle of your day and thank Him. When it is real on the inside of us, it will be real in our responses to Him.

His love has made me alive forevermore. I would be dead with no hope at all had it not been for the Lord. That's why my life should be broadcasting the praises of Jehovah God! He snatched me from the gates of death so that I could praise His Name and follow Him. I was about to be swallowed up, but He stepped in, reached down, and salvaged me. Talk about a rescue operation!

Yes, we have something to shout and sing about. Let's do it with all our hearts!

i will thank the lord

Chorus
I will thank the Lord
With all my heart
I will declare all
Your wonderful works
I will rejoice and boast
About You
And I will sing about Your name
Most High

Verse 1
Consider my affliction
At the hands of my enemies
The gates of death are open
I am balancing
Come steady me

Verse 2
You have not forgotten
The cry of the broken
Their hope will never perish
Your arms are strong
And always open

Written by Margaret Becker & David M. Edwards. ©2005 Modern M/SESAC. Admin. by Music Services, Inc. Van Ness Press/ASCAP. Admin. by LifeWay Worship Music Group.

david m. edwards

David and his wife, Susan, and their three children, have been in ministry for fifteen years, and new songs of worship have been pouring out of him nearly all his life. In 2003, David began "Power to Worship Encounter"—a seminar where attendees not only learn about the nuts and bolts of worship but experience God's presence as well. In 2005, he was awarded *Worship Leader* Magazine's "Best Scripture Song" Praise Award for his song, "Create In Me," featured on his *Faithfully Yours: Psalms* project with Margaret Becker. Truly, this is only the beginning.

For more on David's music and ministry, contact: The Select Artist Group, P. O. Box 1418, LaVergne, Tennessee 37086, www.theselectartistgroup.com. Or visit www.davidmedwards.com.

Besides the other two releases in the *Faithfully Yours* series, David's other books include his signature work, *Worship 365,* as well as his lead editorial work on the *Holman CSB® Personal Worship Bible,* with more to come.

acknowledgments

My sincere appreciation goes to: my publisher, David Shepherd; my literary agent, David Sanford; my editor, Elizabeth Jones, for a phenomenal job and working so quickly; my manager, Glenda J. McNalley, whose tireless efforts on my behalf and unwavering friendship are constant; to my sister and friend, Margaret Becker, your encouragement and creative partnership are a blessing. Our journey continues!

To my beautiful wife, Susan, thank you for your love and standing by my side. *I love you!* Tara, Elyse, and Evan—Daddy loves you so much. To my parents, Louis and Wanda Edwards, and my brother, Daniel, thank you for always being faithful friends.

Lastly, to King David, my sincerest thanks and appreciation for bearing your soul! Thank you for being so sensitive to the Holy Spirit and for not being afraid to tell us how you really felt. Life was not always easy, but you taught us that there is One constant in every circumstance. I am proud to wear your name. Surely you are still writing songs that we will all one day sing!

Information's pretty thin stuff unless mixed with experience.
Clarence Day

FACE TO FACE

An intimate evening of worship with
David M. Edwards and Regi Stone

available at www.experienceworship.com

EXPERIENCE WORSHIP

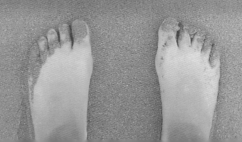